Contents

PUNCTUATION

GRAMMAR

All of the answers can be found online. To get access, simply register or login at **www.risingstars-uk.com.**

1 Sentence punctuation

Sentences begin with a **capital letter** and end with a **full stop (.)**.
If the sentence is a question, it ends with a **question mark (?)**.
If it is an exclamation, it ends with an **exclamation mark (!)**.
Capital letters are also used at the beginning of
proper nouns.

Africa, West Ham United

Activity 1

Rewrite these sentences with the correct punctuation.

.	ABC	?	!

a) we can go out soon

b) where are we going

c) my favourite film is *shrek*

d) that pan is hot – don't touch it

e) can you help me with this please, sally

Activity 2

Rewrite these sentences and add two **full stops** to each line.

a) When we've had our lunch we will go out We'll take a ball and go to the park

b) Snow White got lost in the woods She came across a little cottage

c) They stopped at the red traffic light When it turned green, they carried on

Investigate!

Take some time to check your own writing for correct punctuation. Have you
used **capital letters**, **full stops**, **question marks** and **exclamation marks**?

4

Skills Builders

GRAMMAR AND PUNCTUATION

Nicola Morris

Acknowledgements

ISBN: 978-1-78339-719-8

Text, design and layout © 2016 Rising Stars UK Ltd

First published in 2016 by Rising Stars UK Ltd
Rising Stars UK Ltd, An Hachette UK Company
Carmelite House 50 Victoria Embankment
London EC4Y 0DZ

www.risingstars-uk.com

All facts are correct at time of going to press.

Author: Nicola Morris
Educational Consultant: Madeleine Barnes
Publisher: Laura White
Illustrator: Emily Skinner
Logo design: Amparo Barrera, Kneath Associates Ltd
Design: Julie Martin
Typesetting: Newgen
Cover design: Amparo Barrera, Kneath Associates Ltd
Project Manager: Sarah Bishop, Out of House Publishing
Copy Editor: Hayley Fairhead
Proofreader: Jennie Clifford
Software development: Alex Morris

British Library Cataloguing-in-Publication Data
A CIP record for this book is available from the British Library.
Printed by Liberduplex S.L., Barcelona, Spain

2 Sentence types

There are four different types of sentence.

- A **statement** tells you something and ends with a **full stop**.

  Polar bears live in the Arctic.

- A **question** asks you something and ends with a **question mark**.

  When is your birthday?

- An **exclamation** makes a statement with emotion and ends with an **exclamation mark**.

  What a lovely surprise this is!

- A **command** gives an order and can end with a **full stop** or an **exclamation mark**, depending on how it is said.

  Please collect the books.

  Collect the books!

Activity 1

Label the sentence types below. Write **S** for **statement**, **Q** for **question**, **E** for **exclamation** or **C** for **command**.

a) Tidy your clothes away. _____

b) What's the weather forecast for today? _____

c) How good of you to bring me flowers! _____

d) It's good for your health to eat five portions of fruit and vegetables each day. _____

Activity 2

These are the answers. What are the questions?

a) _____

My favourite colour is blue.

b) _____

I went to Scotland on holiday.

c) _____

I have two brothers and one sister.

3 Using commas

When we write a list, we separate each item with a **comma**. The final two items are separated using **and**, so a **comma** is not needed.

We had sandwiches**,** crisps**,** biscuits **and** fruit on our **picnic**.

We can also write a list of **adjectives** to describe someone or something. Each **adjective** is separated with a **comma** but we don't need to use **and** for this kind of list.

The vast**,** icy**,** grey ocean thundered around the ship.
He stared with wide**,** bulging eyes.

Activity 1

How many **commas** should there be in each of these sentences?

a) We are growing carrots peas tomatoes and potatoes in our garden. _____

b) I love playing hockey netball and tennis. _____

c) Tigers lions elephants and giraffes can all be seen at the zoo. _____

d) The party goody bags contained a balloon some chocolate a small toy a badge and a piece of cake. _____

e) A brilliant dazzling sun burned down. _____

Activity 2

Write down the sentence that has **commas** in the correct place.

a) We will use eggs flour milk and sugar to make a cake today.

b) We will use eggs, flour, milk, and sugar to make a cake today.

c) We will use eggs, flour, milk and sugar to make a cake today.

d) We will use eggs, flour, milk, and, sugar to make a cake today.

Investigate!

Can you write a shopping list showing what you would like to buy if you could choose anything you wanted? You can have five items!

4 Using apostrophes

We use an **apostrophe** to show **contraction** and **possession**.

- **Contraction** is when letters are missing.

  she'd ⟶ she would, haven't ⟶ have not

- **Possession** is when someone owns something. To show **singular possession** (one owner), the **apostrophe** goes before the **s**. To show **plural possession** (more than one owner), the **apostrophe** goes after the **s**.

  Salim**'s** sticker, the dog**'s** collar
  The ant**s'** nest (the nest belongs to many ants)

- An **s** does not need to be added if the plural already ends in an **s**, but it is added if the plural does not end in an **s**.

  The books belonging to the men ⟶ the men**'s** books.

- **Singular proper nouns** ending in an **s** use **'s**.

  Wales**'s** population

SB

Activity 1

Write down whether each **apostrophe** is being used for **contraction** (**C**) or **possession** (**P**). There may be more than one in a sentence.

a) The dogs' kennel is getting too small for them. _____

b) They shouldn't go out in this weather. _____

c) I can't go to Mal's house today because I haven't done my homework. _____
_____

d) Dad's just gone out, so you'll have to wait until he returns. _____ _____

Activity 2

Write down the sentence in each set that shows the correct use of the **apostrophe**.

a) It's time for school.
Its time' for school.
Its' time for school.

b) Tims new scooter' is broken.
Tim's new scooter is broken.
Tims' new scooter is broken.

c) The boy's cant play outside today.
The boys' cant play outside today.
The boys can't play outside today.

Activity 3

Rewrite these sentences, changing the **contractions** into the full words.

a) Roisin doesn't like apples.

b) Joe and Josh said they'd meet us there.

c) We haven't brought our umbrellas because we shouldn't need them.

d) You won't be able to go to the swimming pool today because it's closed.

Activity 4

Rewrite these sentence and change the full words into **contractions**.

a) However hard I try, I cannot do it.

b) We will look after the baby.

c) Tyrell could not go to school today but the doctor says he will be well enough tomorrow.

d) I shall not go to the party!

Activity 5

Who or what do these things belong to? You will need to decide if the **possession** is **singular** or **plural**.

a) Una's cats _____

b) The rabbits' hutch _____

c) The hotel's rooms _____

d) Thomas's football _____

Investigate!

Find examples of where **apostrophes** have been used in books, magazines and newspapers. Decide whether they have been used for **contraction** or **possession**.

5 Conjunctions: or, and, but

A **conjunction** is a word that is used to join sentences. The words **or**, **and** and **but** are **conjunctions**.

Do you want pasta **or** would you prefer rice?
I have visited France **and** I have visited Spain.
They went to the bus stop **but** the bus didn't arrive.

Activity 1

Which **conjunction** makes sense? Choose which one should join these sentences. Rewrite them so that they make one sentence.

> **or**   **and**   **but**

a) Tariq got his bicycle from the shed. He rode to his friend's house.

b) I wanted to buy some bread. The shop was closed.

c) Should we go to the cinema? Should we go to the fair?

d) Milly was going to eat her banana. She had left it at home.

Change these sentences into two sentences using two conjunctions.

We knocked on Luke's door. He didn't answer. Was he in? Was he out?

Activity 2

Rewrite and complete each of these sentences so that they make sense.

a) We got a taxi to the airport and _____.

b) Amy's bedroom was tidy but _____.

c) I wasn't sure if I was wearing suitable clothes or _____.

d) There was just time to have breakfast and _____.

e) She enjoyed the film but _____.

Investigate!

Can you and a partner write sentence openings using **or**, **and**, **but**, and then swap to complete each other's?

9

6 Conjunctions: when, if, that, because

The words **when**, **if**, **that** and **because** are also **conjunctions**. They are used to explain or add information.

Activity 1

Choose the correct **conjunction** to complete each sentence.

| when | if | that | because |

a) We can't go to the museum today _____ it is closed.

b) She is hoping to have tea with us _____ she gets back in time.

c) Portia had a great time _____ she went to the seaside.

d) She couldn't drink her tea straight away _____ it was too hot.

e) Christian was annoyed _____ his brother had taken his game.

f) _____ he arrives, please tell him I couldn't wait _____ I have an appointment.

Activity 2

Which two **conjunctions** make sense in each of these sentences?

a) Freya can buy a magazine _____ she gets her pocket money.

b) Jude was upset _____ his football team had lost.

Investigate!

Can you experiment by using **conjunctions** in your own sentences?

7 Past and present tense

Verbs in the **past tense** tell us about things that have already happened.

She **baked** a cake.

Verbs in the **present tense** tell us about things that are happening now.

She **bakes** a cake.

When we are writing, we need to decide which **tense** we should be using, and use it consistently.

Activity 1

Write down the **verb**(s) in each sentence and whether it is in the **past** or **present** tense. One has been done for you.

He jumped in the playground. Answer: jumped, past tense

a) We travelled to France. _____

b) The children look at their books. _____

c) Salma works on the computer. _____

d) The teacher asked a question. _____

e) She walks to the shops. _____

f) The dog barked loudly and jumped up at his owner. _____ _____

Activity 2

Rewrite each sentence, changing the **tense** from **past** to **present** or **present** to **past**.

a) Oscar played the game.

b) She switched off the light.

c) Someone screams.

d) They all watched television.

e) Ros waits at the bus stop.

f) The little boy cleans his teeth while his mother washes her hands.

8 Verbs in progressive form

The **progressive form** of verbs shows whether the actions are happening now or whether they have happened in the past.

- We can show that actions are happening in the **present tense** by using **am/are/is**.

  I **am running** down the street.
  (The action is in progress.)

- We can show that actions were happening in the **past tense** by using **was/were**.

  I **was running** down the street.
  (The action was in progress.)

Activity 1

Change each sentence from the **past progressive tense** into the **present progressive tense**.

a) Anya was reading a magazine.

b) The gardener was planting some seeds.

c) They were having an argument.

d) The politician was making a speech.

e) We were eating a huge meal.

Activity 2

Change each sentence from the **past tense** into the **past progressive tense** to show that the actions progressed.

a) Zack hopped across the playground.

b) Someone knocked on the door.

c) We listened to the radio.

d) Christy wrote a letter.

e) They took some drinks into the garden.

Investigate!

What is going on around you at the moment? Write sentences in the **present progressive tense** to explain what is happening. Change them to the **past progressive**.

9 Verbs in present perfect form

- We use the **present perfect form** to say that an action has happened at some point in the past, but we don't specify when. We can do this by using **have** or **has** as part of the verb.

  We **have finished** our exams.
  He **has met** a famous football player.

- General time expressions such as **always, never, still, already, before, yet** and **since** can be useful in a **present perfect tense** sentence.

  I have **already** seen that film.

Activity 1

Write down the words that make up the **present perfect tense** in each of these sentences.

a) Ahmed has gone to the shops.

b) We have made sandwiches for our packed lunch.

c) Eva has learned to read.

d) They have played chess.

Activity 2

Rewrite each of these sentences, completing them so that the **verb** is in the **present perfect form**.

a) She _____ always (like) _____ art.

b) Oliver _____ (travel) _____ to America.

c) They _____ (live) _____ here for five years.

d) He _____ already (eat) _____ his breakfast.

e) You _____ (buy) _____ some new clothes.

Investigate!

Can you write sentences in the **present perfect form** about yourself? Use the words **always** and **never** to start you off.

10 Word classes

What can you remember about word classes? We need to know what the word classes are and how we can put them together to form sentences that are grammatically correct.

- A **noun** tells you the name of a thing, place or idea.

  bicycle, America, happiness

- An **adjective** is a describing word.

  ancient, colourful

- A **verb** is a doing or being word.

  shouted, has

- An **adverb** describes a verb, explaining how, when or where something is done.

  earlier, carefully

- A **preposition** works with a noun, to give more information about it by answering the questions **when**, **where** and **why**.

  on, above, before, after, because of

Activity 1

Copy the chart into your book and sort the words below into the correct classes.

Nouns	Adjectives	Verbs	Prepositions

yellow   on   fox   cooked   laughed   nursery   in   young   watched

coat   at   Dubai   over   threw   tiny   carelessness

Activity 2

Rewrite each sentence and circle the word that is a **verb**.

a) Helena walks to school every day.

b) I baked a cake yesterday.

c) In autumn, the leaves fall from the trees.

d) We thought very carefully.

e) Jamie is 10 today.

Activity 3

Which of these words are **nouns**? Write them down and then write a sentence for each one.

| book | read | author | words | enjoy |

a) _____

b) _____

c) _____

Activity 4

Rewrite each sentence, adding two **adjectives** before the underlined **noun**.

Jim drove his <u>car</u>.

Answer: Jim drove his **fast**, **red** car.

a) The <u>baby</u> cried and cried.

b) They had fun at the <u>park</u>.

c) She read a <u>book</u>.

d) Lola walked along the <u>road</u>.

e) He listened to a <u>song</u>.

Investigate!

Can you pick out a sentence in a book and write down the different word classes that you find?

11 Using a or an

The choice of **a** or **an** depends on whether the word after them begins with a consonant or a vowel. When you read them aloud, you will hear that **a** sounds awkward when used before a vowel.

- If the word begins with a consonant, **a** is used.

  a ball, **a** wooden chair

  The word following **a** might be a **noun** or it might be an **adjective**.

- If the word begins with a vowel, **an** is used.

  an umbrella, **an** amazing day

- Exceptions are words with a silent **h**.

  an hour, **an** honourable man

Activity 1

Copy these words into your book and draw lines to show which word (**a** or **an**) goes with each **noun**.

	animal
a	donkey
	panda
	elephant
an	otter
	tiger
	kangaroo

Activity 2

You will see that **a** and **an** are missing from these sentences. Rewrite them, deciding which is the correct word to use.

a) Louisa went for walk.

b) Jaden played with orange ball.

c) I ate jacket potato at lunchtime.

d) We saw alligator.

e) She fell off slide and ambulance came.

f) They watched football match and bought programme.

2 Using determiners

A **determiner** goes with a **noun** to modify it, or to give the reader more information about which noun is being talked about.

- They can be the articles **a**, **an** and **the**.
- They can demonstrate which noun is being talked about, using **this**, **that**, **these**, **those**.
- They can be **possessive**, telling us who the noun belongs to, such as **its**, **our**, **their**, **my**, **your**, **his**, **her**.
- They can tell us how many or how much, using **all**, **some**, **few**, **both**, **many**, **every**, **little**, **two**, **three**, **four** or any number.

Activity 1

Which are the **determiners** in these sentences?

a) I would like those bananas, please. _____

b) That coat belongs to me. _____

c) Every time we go out, the baby cries. _____ _____

d) There is not enough milk to put on our cereal. _____ _____

e) I need to go to the supermarket to get some ingredients to make three cakes.
_____ _____ _____

Activity 2

Rewrite each sentence using the correct **determiner**.

| little | the | this | their | all | an | few |

a) I'll bring _____ umbrella, in case it rains.

b) _____ is the t-shirt I want to buy.

c) Dad likes a _____ milk in his tea.

d) Make sure you put _____ of the rubbish in the bin.

e) We'll buy a _____ sweets to eat on _____ journey to _____ house.

13 Using adverbs

Adverbs work with the **verb** in a sentence. They can explain how something is done. Many of these have an **ly** ending.

slow**ly**, quiet**ly**

There are exceptions.

You're working **hard** today.

Activity 1

Decide which word from each set is an **adverb**.

a) spoke	happy	angrily	country	_____
b) unkindly	beautiful	cried	peace	_____
c) shouting	closely	friendship	but	_____
d) fast	shiny	apply	magical	_____
e) careless	frightened	butterfly	carelessly	_____

Activity 2

Identify and write the **adverb** in each of these sentences. Then rewrite the sentence with the **adverb** in a different place. Check that it makes sense.

The man ate the crisps **noisily**. *or* The man **noisily** ate the crisps.
or **Noisily**, the man ate the crisps.

a) She read the important letter carefully.

_____

b) He ate his meal hungrily.

_____

c) The train noisily arrived at the station.

_____

d) Everyone arrived suddenly.

_____

4 Using adverbs to show when, where or why

As well as being used to explain how and how often an action happens, **adverbs** can also answer the questions **when, where** or **why**. They can be used at the beginning, middle or end of sentences. Some **adverbs** do a similar job to **conjunctions**.

She painted her picture **carefully**.

I get a lift to school **sometimes**.

Then, we went to get a drink.

Hanging **above** me was a spider's web.

Therefore, we will have to go shopping.

Activity 1

Which question is answered by the **adverb** (or phrase) underlined in each sentence? Write **when, where** or **why**.

a) <u>Sometimes</u>, we buy an ice-cream after school.

b) A police officer was standing <u>nearby</u>.

c) Children were running around <u>everywhere</u>.

d) We visit the dentist <u>regularly</u>.

e) I always do my homework <u>because I want to do well at school</u>.

Activity 2

Choose the correct **adverb** to complete each sentence.

> **before**   **long ago**   **here**   **usually**   **since**

a) _____, there lived a wicked queen.

b) Put your coat on _____ you go out.

c) They _____ visit their grandparents at the weekend.

d) We've been camping a lot _____ we bought our new tent.

e) _____ is the shop we're looking for.

Activity 3

Change the **adverb** for a different one that also makes sense. Rewrite the sentence using your chosen **adverb**.

a) Keira **often** runs in the park.

b) **Then** I walked to my friend's house.

c) Please go **upstairs** to get your jumper.

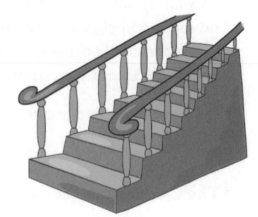

d) You will need to come home **soon**.

e) They have gone **inside**.

Activity 4

Decide which word from each set is an **adverb**.

a) haunted   next   our   old   _____

b) frequent   frequently   red   nest   _____

c) down   egg   hopeful   found   _____

d) his   plane   only   when   _____

e) above   went   I   pebble   _____

Investigate!

Find **adverbs** from books in the classroom or library and decide which question they answer: **when, where** or **why**.

15 Using conjunctions

Conjunctions are used to extend sentences and give extra information. They provide a link that answers the questions **when** and **why**. They can be used at the beginning or in the middle of sentences.

The teacher was happy **when** the children had done their homework.

The cat was hungry **because** he had missed his breakfast.

Before we go out, we need to get our umbrellas.

Always check that your sentence makes sense.

Activity 1

Write down the information that the underlined **conjunction** helps to tell you. Does it show **when** the action happened or **why** the action happened?

a) We went to the supermarket <u>so</u> we could buy some fruit. _____

b) <u>After</u>, Zahra did her homework. _____

c) Meishan went to the doctor's <u>because</u> she had a sore throat. _____

d) She did a crossword <u>while</u> she was waiting. _____

e) They had to wait <u>until</u> the shop opened. _____

Activity 2

Choose the correct **conjunction** to complete each sentence.

| so | when | as | by the time | meanwhile |

a) We'll cross the road _____ we find a safe place.

b) _____, Bob was watching television in the other room.

c) Dean wanted to buy a new game _____ he was saving his pocket money.

d) _____ we arrived, the film had already started.

e) The fish are hungry _____ I forgot to feed them.

16 Using prepositions

A **preposition** links a **noun** or **pronoun** to another word or phrase in a sentence. They can be used to answer the questions **when, where** and **why**. You will notice that some **prepositions** have already appeared as **conjunctions** or **adverbs**. When a word is working as a **preposition**, it is giving more information about a **noun** or **pronoun**.

We will meet **before** lunch.

He took some money **out** of his wallet.

She felt carsick **because** of the winding roads.

Activity 1

Copy the chart into your book and sort the **prepositions** below to show which question they answer – **when** or **where**?

| over | by | since | behind | until | near | around | meanwhile | through |

When?	Where?

Activity 2

Write down the **preposition(s)** used in each of these sentences.

a) The cow jumped over the moon. _____

b) There was a library nearby. _____

c) They went for a swim at the pool. _____

d) Oliver likes to play all sports except rugby. _____

e) The children were walking towards us. _____

f) Humpty Dumpty sat on a wall and then fell off the wall. _____ _____

Activity 3

Choose the correct **preposition** to complete each sentence.

during	up	because of	beside	against
	despite	last	after	

a) It had rained _____ the night.

b) The plane couldn't land _____ the stormy weather.

c) We will eat at the restaurant _____ the film.

d) Joanna was determined to go out _____ her illness.

e) She has a lamp on a table _____ her bed.

f) _____ night, Malachi put the ladder _____ the wall and then climbed _____.

Activity 4

Write one **preposition** that can complete both sentences in each pair.

a) Put the knives and forks _____ the table.

The sun shone _____ the mountain.

b) Justine is standing _____ to Yusra.

We can come back _____ week.

c) The boat sailed _____ the bridge.

He wore a shirt _____ his jacket.

d) The map showed a right turn just _____ the park.

You must do the washing-up _____ you can go out.

Investigate!

Can you use **prepositions** to help you to describe what you can see around the classroom?

17 Subordinate clauses

A **main clause** is a group of words with a **subject** and a **verb** that can stand on its own, making a **simple sentence**.

The man took his dog for a walk.

A **subordinate clause** tells us more about the **main clause**. It cannot stand alone. A **main clause** and a **subordinate clause** go together to make a **complex sentence**.

The man took his dog for a walk **because it was such a beautiful day.**

Conjunctions such as **when, before, after, while, so, because** and **unless** are used to show **subordinate clauses**. They can be used at the beginning or in the middle of a sentence.

The man took his dog for a walk **because** it was such a beautiful day.

Because it was such a beautiful day, the man took his dog for a walk.

Activity 1

Rewrite each sentence and then underline the **subordinate clause**.

a) We'll go to the cinema because they're showing a new film.

b) It's great at the beach when the sun is shining.

c) Finn will go to Spain if he can save enough money.

d) She'll do some work after she's eaten her tea.

e) He ran out of milk so he had to go to the shop.

Activity 2

Choose your own **conjunction** to complete each sentence.

a) Libraries are great for readers _____ they are free.

b) _____ it rains, we need to take in the washing.

c) I'm going to stay in bed _____ my alarm goes off.

d) Libby wanted a good seat for the concert _____ she booked her ticket early.

e) _____ you don't tell me, I won't know what you want to do.

Activity 3

Decide whether the underlined clauses are **main clauses** or **subordinate clauses**. Write down **M** (main) or **S** (subordinate).

a) Keep watering the plants <u>so that they grow.</u>

b) After you've tidied your bedroom, <u>you can watch television</u>.

c) <u>Although you weren't very hungry,</u> you've finished your tea.

d) <u>Jon cleaned the car</u> because he wanted to earn some money.

e) Faozia loved to write <u>whenever she had the time</u>.

Activity 4

Add your own **main clause** to each of these **subordinate clauses**.

a) _____ because we needed new school clothes.

b) _____ while we ate our tea.

c) When Cerys arrived home, _____.

d) Before you go swimming, _____.

e) _____ so you don't forget to take it.

f) If you are feeling better, _____.

Investigate!

Can you work with a partner to practise writing sentences with **subordinate clauses?** Write down a **simple sentence** (such as *The cat went outside*). Your partner has to ask you a question about it (such as *Why did the cat go outside?*), and then you can add that information (such as *The cat went outside because it wanted some exercise*). Then swap over.

18 Adding prefixes

Prefixes are used to change the meaning of a word.

- The **prefixes un**, **in**, **dis** and **mis** all have negative meanings.

  finished ⟶ **un**finished, active ⟶ **in**active,
  like ⟶ **dis**like, fortune ⟶ **mis**fortune

- The **prefix anti** means 'against'.

  septic ⟶ **anti**septic

- The **prefix auto** means 'self' or 'own'.

  biography ⟶ **auto**biography

- The **prefix super** means 'greater'.

  market ⟶ **super**market

- The **prefix re** means 'again' or 'back'.

  fresh ⟶ **re**fresh

Activity 1

Choose the correct **prefix** (**un**, **in** or **dis**) to change these words into their opposites.

a) convenient   correct   sincere   _____

b) happy   pleasant   breakable   _____

c) agree   trust   appear   _____

Activity 2

Choose the correct **prefix** so that each sentence makes sense.

     anti   **mis**   **auto**   **un**   **re**   **in**   **dis**

a) The jigsaw was _____complete as one of the pieces was missing.

b) _____cycle your plastic bottles to help the environment.

c) There was a long queue of people waiting to get the actor's _____graph.

d) They ran in an _____clockwise direction around the field.

e) The girl's parents were _____pleased with her _____behaviour as they hadn't expected her to be so _____kind to others.

19 Changing singular nouns to plural nouns

The rules for making **plurals** are given below.

- For most words, just add **s**.
  boat ——→ boat**s**, garden ——→ garden**s**
- For words that end **ss**, **sh**, **ch** or **x**, add **es**.
  bush ——→ bush**es**, witch ——→ witch**es**
- For words that end in **y**, change **y** to **i** before adding **es**, unless there's a vowel before the **y**.
  baby ——→ bab**ies** *but* tray ——→ tray**s**
- For most words that end in **f** or **fe**, change the **f** to **ves**.
  scarf ——→ scar**ves**
- Some plurals are irregular and just have to be learned.
  woman ——→ **women**, child ——→ **children**,
  mouse ——→ **mice**

Activity 1

Write down the sentence in each pair that has the correct **plural**.

a) She set the table with knifes and forks.
She set the table with knives and forks.

b) There were red berries on the bush.
There were red berrys on the bush.

c) They were sure that foxs had been in their garden.
They were sure that foxes had been in their garden.

Activity 2

Use the rules to help you to decide how to change the noun from **singular** to **plural**.

a) In the summer, there can sometimes be a lot of (fly) _____.

b) I'm making (sandwich) _____ to take on our trip.

c) Young children might ride (donkey) _____ on the beach.

d) On the farm, the cows were looking after their (calf) _____.

e) Before he went to bed, Ash cleaned his (tooth) _____.

Investigate!

What can you see more than one of around you? Write down all the **plural** nouns you can see.

20 Using headings and sub-headings

Headings and **sub-headings** help us to organise non-fiction writing so that it is clear to follow.

- A **heading** is the title at the top of a page or section of a book.
- **Sub-headings** are used to break up the information under the **heading**. The **sub-headings** will be related to the **heading**.

Activity 1

Choose the three **sub-headings** that would be appropriate for the heading 'Teeth'.

Different types	**Keeping them warm**	**My favourite**
Rules for playing	**Chewing**	**Looking after them**

Choose the three **sub-headings** that would be appropriate for the heading 'New York'.

Playing the guitar	**Buildings**	**The skeleton**
Food	**How to make a chocolate cake**	**Languages**

Activity 2

Put the following sentences in the order they would be written under the **heading** and **sub-heading**.

Heading: Sports for children
Sub-heading: Rounders

a) It is a bat and ball game played between two teams.

b) Rounders was first played in Tudor times.

c) Points are called 'rounders' and are scored by running around four posts.

Investigate!

Can you think of **sub-headings** to match a topic you are learning about at school?

21 Use of Standard English

We write using **Standard English**, which means choosing the correct forms so that everyone is writing in the same way. When using the verb 'to be' in the past tense, **Standard English** follows these rules.

I was
You were
He/she/it was
We were
They were

- Make sure you use the verb form **we were** instead of **we was**.

- Make sure you use the verb form **I did** instead of **I done**. If you are using 'done', it needs 'have' before it.

  I did my homework.
  I have done my homework.

- Know when to use **I** and when to use **me**. To check that you have chosen correctly from **I** and **me**, take out the other person in the sentence and see if it makes sense.

Activity 1

Rewrite each sentence, choosing the correct verb form from **was** or **were**.

a) I _____ looking forward to my birthday.

b) They _____ walking to school.

c) We _____ going to watch cricket, but the match was cancelled.

d) He _____ eating his tea.

Write a sentence of your own, starting with: **I was/You were/She was/We were** or **They were**.

_____

_____

Activity 2

Rewrite each sentence, choosing the correct verb form from **did** or **have done**.

a) I _____ all of my homework before tea.

b) You _____ your chores.

c) I _____ the washing-up.

d) They _____ the best work they could.

Write two sentences of your own, checking that they make sense.

e) We did _____ .

f) They have done _____ .

Activity 3

Rewrite each sentence, choosing **I** or **me** to complete them correctly.

a) Ruby and _____ gave out the books.

b) Mum took Declan and _____ to the cinema.

c) Madeline and _____ bought Adele a present.

d) At the fair, Nikolas and _____ went
on the dodgems.

e) Grandad asked Marcus and _____ to go
shopping for him.

Investigate!

Find examples of the use of **I** and **me** from books, or even from listening to what people around you say.

22 Irregular verb families

There are a lot of **irregular** verbs in the English language, which means that they do not follow a pattern.

- **To be** – I am/I was; you are/you were; it is/it was; we are/we were; you are/you were; they are/they were
- **To have** – I have/I had; you have/you had; it has/it had; we have/we had; you have/you had; they have/they had
- **To do** – I do/I did; you do/you did; it does/it did; we do/we did; you do/you did; they do/they did
- **To take** – I take/I took; you take/you took; it takes/it took; we take/we took; you take/you took; they take/they took
- The verbs **to go**, **to come**, **to make**, **to say**, and **to write** are also **irregular**.

Activity 1

Choose the correct verb form to complete each sentence.

ate   wore   found   won   came   lit

a) Last night, we _____ fish and chips.

b) A hundred people _____ to the wedding.

c) Caroline _____ her new coat.

d) He _____ the race.

e) The lamp _____ up the whole room.

f) Dragosh _____ the missing ring.

Activity 2

Change these **irregular verbs** from the **present tense** to the **past tense**.

a) Mum <u>takes</u> Robbie to school.

b) We <u>make</u> a model from junk materials.

c) Alex <u>writes</u> a letter.

d) The teacher <u>speaks</u> to the class.

e) Hulya <u>pays</u> the cashier.

23 Types of noun

Nouns are naming words. There are different types of **noun**.

- A **common noun** names a general person, place or thing.

  girl, apple, city

- A **proper noun** names a specific person, place or thing. All proper nouns start with a capital letter

  Elizabeth, Saturday, Manchester, The Gruffalo

- An **abstract noun** names something that you might not be able to see, but is an idea, feeling or quality.

  imagination, anger, bravery

- A **collective noun** describes a number of animals or objects.

  a gaggle of geese, a litter of kittens

Activity 1

Decide which of these are **proper nouns**. Rewrite them, making sure that they begin with a **capital letter**.

dinosaur   tuesday   diwali   table   july

harry potter   despicable me   christmas   car   birthday

charlotte   school   italy   eid   supermarket

Activity 2

Choose the most appropriate **abstract noun** to fit in each sentence, or use an idea of your own.

honesty   courage   friendship   jealousy

a) She was overcome with _____ when someone else won the prize.

b) Mark had known Nathan for five years and really valued his _____.

c) He showed his _____ when he handed in the money he found.

d) As she stood at the edge of the pool, she knew she would need all of her _____ to jump in.

Activity 3

Rewrite each sentence and underline the **noun** or **nouns**.

a) Tomas looked out of the window.

b) The playground was full of children playing cricket, rounders and football.

c) Miss McCarthy was reading *Billionaire Boy* by David Walliams to her class.

d) Victoria Park Swimming Pool is closed on Mondays.

e) Melissa took her friends to a soft-play centre on her birthday.

f) She couldn't believe her luck when she won a prize.

Activity 4

Match the collective word to its **noun**. One has been done for you.

herd   sheep

swarm   fish

flock   lions

pack   cows

school   bees

pride   wolves

Investigate!

List all of the nouns that you can see around you. This might include **proper nouns**, such as the names of your friends and titles of books. You might also see some **abstract nouns**, including the qualities you see in other people, such as **concentration** or **friendship**.

24 Expanded noun phrases

A **noun phrase** is a group of words that work together and contain a **noun**.

the dog

An **expanded noun phrase** gives more detail about the **noun**.

the dog with the loud bark

We have added an **adjective** 'loud' and a **noun** 'bark'.

the huge, shaggy dog in his kennel

We have added **adjectives** 'huge', 'shaggy' and a **prepositional phrase** to say exactly which dog we are talking about and where he is 'in his kennel'.

All these things make your writing more interesting and help the reader to build up a picture in their mind.

Activity 1

Write down three different **adjectives** to go with each of these **nouns**.

a) car _____ _____ _____

b) party _____ _____ _____

c) chair _____ _____ _____

d) football match _____ _____ _____

e) palace _____ _____ _____

Activity 2

Rewrite and then complete each phrase by choosing an appropriate **noun**.

a) the young child with the curly _____

b) an ancient book with torn _____

c) the sleek cat with a silver _____

d) a block of flats with broken _____

e) her new dress with purple _____

Activity 3

Where could the **noun** be? Rewrite the **noun phrase** and add your own **prepositional phrase**.

this little box **on the table**

a) a tall tree _____

b) the aeroplane _____

c) that small child _____

d) those sticky sweets _____

e) some dark clouds _____

Activity 4

Choose a word or phrase from each column to create as many different **expanded noun phrases** as you can.

a hopeful footballer with pale blue eyes

Determiner	Adjective	Noun	Preposition phrase
a	strict	father	with golden hair
an	hopeful	teacher	with the muscly arms
the	excited	gardener	with pale blue eyes
my	swift	princess	with an evil glare
their	cheerful	footballer	with the freckled nose
that	frightened	witch	with a large nose

Investigate!

Who can you see around you? Use **expanded noun phrases** to describe the children in your class, and your teachers!

25 Using nouns and pronouns

Pronouns are used to replace a **noun** within a sentence to avoid repetition.

Tom grabbed Tom's coat ⟶ Tom grabbed **his** coat.

Personal pronouns such as **I**, **me**, **she** and **they** replace names of people or things.

Possessive pronouns such as **my**, **mine**, **their**, **our**, **his**, **her** and **its** tell us who or what something belongs to.

Some pronouns are not specific about who or what is being talked about, such as **something**, **nothing**, **everyone** and **anything**.

Activity 1

Which is the **pronoun** in each of these sentences?

a) He read a book. _____

b) Gina and I went to the cinema. _____

c) Kim gave everyone one of her home-made cookies. _____ _____

d) The teacher asked them to bring their PE kits to school. _____ _____

e) Please give it to me, it's mine! _____ _____ _____

Activity 2

Write the **pronoun(s)** you could use to avoid repetition.

a) Amelia walked to her friend's house. <u>Amelia</u> knocked on the door. _____

b) Junior and Chandon went out hunting bugs. <u>Junior and Chandon</u> found some ladybirds in a bush. _____

c) Kate and Rose were in <u>Kate and Rose's</u> bedroom. _____

d) Mariam picked up <u>Mariam's</u> bag. _____

e) Grandma and Grandpa came to stay and I showed <u>Grandma and Grandpa</u> to <u>Grandma and Grandpa's</u> room. _____ _____

Activity 3

Identify and write down the **pronouns** in each sentence.

a) Everybody voted to have five minutes extra at playtime.

b) When Chloe opened the door, nobody was there.

c) They could hear the footsteps of someone outside.

d) Kamil said he didn't want anything to eat.

e) The children had to agree on something to get Dad.

Activity 4

Rewrite each of these sentences, completing them by choosing the correct **pronoun**.

    your   **she**   **my**   **his**   **anyone**   **their**   **something**

a) Mario took _____ dog for a walk.

b) I cleaned _____ teeth before bed.

c) Danisa and Mia will drive in _____ own car.

d) You will need to collect _____ coat from the cloakroom.

e) When he felt hungry, Kamil would get _____ to eat.

f) When Paige got home, _____ went straight to her room without telling _____.

Investigate!

How many different **pronouns** can you find? Make a list when you look at books in your book corner or library.

26 Fronted adverbials

An **adverbial** is a word or phrase that is used to give more information about a **verb** or **clause**. It can answer the questions **how**, **when**, **where** and **how often**.

The nurse put on the bandage **with great care**.

When I got up, I had my breakfast.

At the airport, we checked our luggage in.

Adverbials can be used at the beginning, in the middle or at the end of sentences. When they are at the beginning (or front) of a sentence, they are called **fronted adverbials**. We generally put a **comma** after a **fronted adverbial**.

In the middle of the night, I went downstairs.

Activity 1

Write down the **fronted adverbial** in each of these sentences.

a) Yesterday evening, we all watched television together.

b) Along the seashore, we collected shells.

c) All of a sudden, the birds started to sing.

d) Every Friday afternoon, Miss Nawaz takes her class swimming.

e) If there is time, you can choose another book.

Activity 2

Rewrite each sentence, putting the **comma** in the correct place.

a) In August we are going on holiday.

b) When the alarm went off I jumped out of bed.

c) During the lunch break we all played football.

d) So long as you bring your kit you can do PE.

e) Every time you move your chair it makes a scraping noise.

Activity 3

Match the **fronted adverbials** to their endings and write the sentences down.

Under the tree,	a plane was taking off.
When everyone arrives,	the dog started barking loudly.
Due to the bad weather,	they shared a picnic.
Millions of years ago,	we can take the register.
In the distance,	the match has been cancelled.
Without warning,	dinosaurs became extinct.

Activity 4

Rewrite each sentence, putting the **adverbial** at the front. One has been done for you.

I packed my suitcase **with great excitement** ⟶ **With great excitement,** I packed my suitcase.

a) A ghost appeared in front of them.

b) Patricia checked that she had everything she needed before she left the house.

c) I like to visit the Science Museum when I'm in London.

d) Cameron put on a hat so that he wouldn't get cold.

e) The engineers were mending the water pipes beside the road.

f) We meet up for lunch once in a while.

Investigate!

Can you experiment with putting different **adverbials** at the beginning of sentences? Start with the **adverbials** in this unit, completing them with your own sentence endings.

27 Direct speech

Direct speech is what the speaker actually says. We place **inverted commas** around the words that are being spoken. Any punctuation at the end of those words also needs to be inside the inverted commas.

"Don't forget your school bag," said Mum.

"I'll huff and I'll puff and I'll blow your house down," said the Big Bad Wolf.

Activity 1

Rewrite the sentences with **inverted commas** around the words that are being spoken, including the punctuation at the end of the speech.

a) We're going out in five minutes, said Mum.

b) Please can I have a cake? asked Susannah.

c) I will give you three wishes, said the Fairy Godmother.

d) My knee is really hurting, screamed the little girl.

Activity 2

Put the words in each speech bubble in **inverted commas** and then say who was speaking.

a)

This certificate is for your fantastic work this week!

_____

_____

said _____

b)

Do you want to play football?

_____

_____

said _____

8 Direct speech: punctuation

We know that we use **inverted commas** to show **direct speech**, but we also need to use other punctuation when writing **dialogue**.

- **Direct speech** begins with a **capital letter**.
- There should always be a **comma, exclamation mark** or **question mark** before the inverted comma at the end of the **direct speech**.
- Whenever there is a new speaker, start a new line.

Activity 1

Write down the sentence that has all of the correct punctuation for **direct speech**.

"Remember to clean your teeth twice a day" said the dentist.

"Remember to clean your teeth twice a day," said the dentist.

"remember to clean your teeth twice a day," said the dentist.

"Remember to clean your teeth twice a day, said the dentist.

Activity 2

Rewrite each sentence, putting in the correct speech punctuation. Remember **inverted commas, commas, question marks** and **exclamation marks**.

a) I'm really enjoying this programme exclaimed Raheem.

b) Please take a seat in the waiting room said the receptionist.

c) Excuse me, can you tell me the way to the library? asked Jamelia.

d) I challenge you to a race said the hare to the tortoise.

Investigate!

Can you write your own **dialogue**? You could add **dialogue** to a story you've written before. Check that you have used the correct punctuation.

29 Plural and possessive

Using **s** at the end of a **noun** has two purposes.

- The **s** can show a **plural**.

  hamster**s**, buse**s**

- The **s** can show **possession**.

  Lena**'s** computer, the babie**s'** bottles

You will notice that an **apostrophe** is used to show **possession** only. An **apostrophe** is not used to show a **plural**.

Activity 1

Copy the chart into your book and put a tick in the correct column to show which words have **s** because they are **plural** and which have **s** because they show **possession**.

Word	's' to show plural	's' to show possession
sisters		
sister's		
sisters'		
brothers		

Activity 2

Choose the correct word to complete each sentence.

a) All of the _____ were playing football. (boys/boy's/boys')

b) The _____ drink dripped on the table. (girls/girl's/girls')

c) _____ nightmare woke her up. (Simones/Simone's/Simones')

d) He put the _____ in a pile. (boxes/box's/boxes')

e) The _____ playground was closed. (childrens/children's/childrens')

Investigate!

Can you find words with **s** in books in your book corner or library, and decide if they show a **plural** or to show **possession**?

0 Paragraphs

A **paragraph** is made up of a collection of sentences that are about the same thing. **Paragraphs** help us to organise our writing and make it easier to read. We leave a line between **paragraphs**, so that it is clear that we are changing ideas.

Activity 1

Sort the sentences below so that they belong to the **paragraph** on the correct theme. Copy the chart into your book and write the letter of the sentence in the correct place.

Paragraph 1: Invasion	Paragraph 2: Roads	Paragraph 3: Soldiers

a) Only men could be in the Roman army.

b) In 55BC, Julius Caesar wanted to conquer Britain and extend the Roman Empire.

c) The Celts used paths and tracks to connect local farms.

d) The Romans wanted to be able to send troops and supplies to different areas of the country.

e) They wore armour made from strips of iron and leather.

f) After winning several battles, Julius Caesar returned to France.

g) Emperor Claudius organised the third, successful invasion of Britain.

h) The Fosse Way ran from Exeter to Lincoln.

i) They usually fought in lines, marching forward with their shields facing the enemy.

In this example, two children go out into the woods one day.

Sort the following sentences so that they belong to the **paragraph** on the correct theme. Copy the chart below into your book and write the letter of the sentence in the correct place.

Paragraph 1: Into the woods	Paragraph 2: Lost	Paragraph 3: Finding the way

a) In the woods, it became darker and darker.

b) They didn't look back.

c) One sunny morning, Evie and Jon set off to explore the woods.

d) Eventually, they saw daylight and ran towards it.

e) The tall trees seemed to whisper menacingly around them.

f) They didn't know which way to go.

g) They laughed as they twisted and turned through the trees.

h) In the distance, they could see their family, still where they had left them.

i) Excited, they ran towards a path, which seemed to be an entrance.

Investigate!

Can you plan out the **paragraphs** of your own story by thinking of themes to take you from the beginning to the end?

1 Terminology check

You've been practising terminology (special words) from Year 2 and Year 3, and new terminology for Year 4. Let's see what you can remember. If there's anything you're unsure about, you can have a look back through this book.

Activity 1

Match up the words on the left with the definitions on the right.

conjunction	tells us exactly which noun we are talking about
adverbial	replaces a noun within a sentence
preposition	links clauses or ideas
expanded noun phrase	shows when, where or why a verb happened
determiner	gives more information about the noun
pronoun	explains when or where a noun is

Activity 2

Write down the word to make or complete the **verb** in each of these sentences.

a) Jen _____ listening to the radio while she washed her hair.

b) At the moment, Hannah _____ shopping.

c) My brother _____ always hated peas.

d) We _____ planning to go to town yesterday.

e) Now, the children _____ playing in the sandpit.

Activity 3

Write down the letters of the sentences that are punctuated correctly. Rewrite the others, correcting them. Look carefully as there might be more than one mistake!

a) i can't wait to go on holiday

b) "Thank you for the present," said Ashley.

c) Would you like a sandwich?

d) Don't touch that

e) "Can I go to Joes house asked Rod.

f) Earlier that day Carlton had made breakfast for everyone.

Name five different types of punctuation that you have used in this activity.

Activity 4

Write a word from the word class shown in brackets so that each sentence makes sense.

a) We are looking forward to visiting _____ tomorrow. (proper noun)

b) Please put the shopping _____. (preposition)

c) Ravi wanted to have his hair cut _____ he went on holiday. (conjunction)

d) She put the _____ book back on the shelf. (adjective)

e) Rob and Angela are having a party at _____ house. (pronoun)

f) I would like _____ sweet, please. (determiner)

Activity 5

a) Choose the correct **plural** from each pair.

lorries	lorrys
churchs	churches
shelfs	shelves
mice	mouses

b) Complete each of these sentences, using an **apostrophe** to show **possession**. The first one has been done for you.

The bat belongs to Joe, so it's **Joe's bat**.

The bedroom belongs to the twins, so it's _____.

The library belongs to the school, so it's _____.

The computer belongs to the children, so it's _____.

c) Write the **contraction** for each of these, using an **apostrophe**.

cannot _____

he is _____

they were _____

will not _____

d) What would you use under a **heading** to help you to organise your non-fiction writing?

_____

Investigate!

What are you confident about using now? What do you think you need to practise a little more?